William Shakespeare

By Charlotte Allin

Series Literacy Consultant
Dr Ros Fisher

Pearson Education Limited
Edinburgh Gate
Harlow
Essex CM20 2JE
England

www.longman.co.uk

The rights of Charlotte Allin to be identified as the author of this Work have been asserted by her in accordance with the Copyright, Designs and Patents Act, 1988.

Text Copyright © 2004 Pearson Education Limited. Compilation Copyright © 2004 Dorling Kindersley Ltd. All rights reserved. No part of this publication may be reproduced, stored in a retrieval system or transmitted in any form or by any means electronic, mechanical, photocopying, recording, or otherwise, without either the prior written permission of the publishers and copyright owners or a licence permitting restricted copying in the United Kingdom issued by the Copyright Licensing Agency Ltd., 90 Tottenham Court Road, London W1P 9HE

ISBN 0 582 84157 7

Colour reproduction by Colourscan, Singapore
Printed and bound in China by Leo Paper Products Ltd.

The Publisher's policy is to use paper manufactured from sustainable forests.

10 9 8 7 6 5 4 3

The following people from **DK** have
contributed to the development of this product:

Art Director Rachael Foster
Martin Wilson **Managing Art Editor** | **Managing Editor** Marie Greenwood
Clair Watson **Design** | **Editorial** Marian Broderick
Brenda Clynch **Picture Research** | **Production** Gordana Simakovic
Richard Czapnik, Andy Smith **Cover Design** | **DTP** David McDonald
Consultant Nick Robins

Dorling Kindersley would like to thank: Rose Horridge, Hayley Smith and Gemma Woodward in the DK Picture Library; Selina Wood and Elise See Tai for editorial assistance; Becky Painter for design assistance; and Johnny Pau for additional cover design work.

Picture Credits: AKG London: 12b; Erich Lessing 8cr. Bridgeman Art Library, London/New York: 26br; Corpus Christi College, Cambridge, UK 15cl; National Museums of Scotland 8bl; O'Shea Gallery, London UK 10b; Private Collection 4b, 15tr, 23tr, Shakespeare's signature; Sotheby's, New York, USA 16bl. By Permission of the Trustees of Dulwich Picture Gallery: 25tr. Donald Cooper/Photostage: 14b, 15br, 17b, 25b, 27bl. Corbis: 4tr; Robert Estall 9b. DK Images: Tony Barton Collection 21cl; British Library 13tr, 13cr; British Museum 13bcr, 13cbr; Weald and Downland Open Air Museum 6tl; York Archaeological Trust 7tl. Peter Earthy: 19tr. Mary Evans Picture Library: 9tr, 10tl, 12tl, 27tr. Robert Harding Picture Library: 28t. Moviestore Collection: 24bl, 30bl; Warner 30cr. National Portrait Gallery, London: 1. Photographic Survey, Courtauld Institute of Art: Private Collection 17tr. The Picture Desk: Kobal Collection 30cl. Public Record Office: 28bl. Shakespeare Birthplace Trust Records Office: 5tr, 5b, 6b, 7bl. Shakespeare's Globe: 30tl, 30cla, 30cal; Donald Cooper 29tr; Richard Kalina 18–19; John Tramper 20tl, 20br.
Cover: Corbis: front bl. Public Record Office: front background.

All other images: Dorling Kindersley © 2004. For further information see www.dkimages.com
Dorling Kindersley Ltd., 80 Strand, London WC2R ORL

Contents

Meeting Shakespeare	4
The Early Years	5
London Bound	10
On Stage	17
The King's Men	23
Timeline	31
Index	32

Meeting Shakespeare

William Shakespeare (1564–1616)

Sixteenth-century London was a vibrant city, full of opportunity for a young man with a great ambition to act and write. Enter William Shakespeare.

Shakespeare is the most famous English writer who ever lived. Every year hundreds of thousands of people from all over the world flock to his birthplace and the site of his grave.

Shakespeare is known for the power and poetry of his language. It may surprise people to know that they are quoting Shakespeare when they say a person is "as gentle as a lamb", or when they tell someone to "go like lightning".

For hundreds of years, Shakespeare's plays have been performed across the globe, and he is still as popular today.

Shakespeare's signature

The Early Years

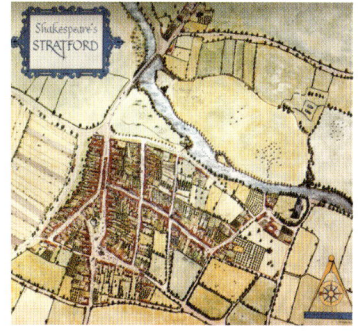

Stratford-upon-Avon lies in the heart of England.

William Shakespeare was born in April 1564 in the small English market town of Stratford-upon-Avon. His father, John, was a respected glove-maker, and a leading member of the community.

Shakespeare's mother, Mary Arden, was a farmer's daughter. Their first two children, a boy and a girl, died while still babies. Infant deaths were common at this time, as there were few medicines to fight illnesses. It must have been a great joy to John and Mary when their third child, William, was born healthy and strong.

Shakespeare was born in this house in Henley Street, Stratford-upon-Avon.

Many large families used trundle beds like this one.

According to church records, William Shakespeare was christened on 26th April in 1564. His birthday is traditionally celebrated on 23rd April, though Shakespeare's actual birth date remains a mystery.

Five more babies followed William, but sadly, one died while still a baby. The family grew up in a comfortable, but rather crowded home. William probably shared a bed with one or two of his brothers. On cold nights, they'd have been glad to huddle together for warmth.

This room is probably where William and his brothers and sisters were born.

A horn book had a wooden frame, with a sheet of paper covered by a thin layer of transparent horn. This one is written in Latin.

It is believed that Shakespeare went to "petty" school when he was about four. There he would have been taught to read using a horn book that showed the alphabet and combinations of letters, such as "ab eb ib ob ub".

When he was about six or seven, William probably started school in Stratford. Shakespeare's father was important in the town, so it is likely that Shakespeare would have studied at the local grammar school – the King's New School of Stratford-upon-Avon, as it was then known.

As a small schoolboy at "petty" school, William would have sat on a stool, much like this, to read and write.

As an older boy, Shakespeare was probably taught in this school room.

>
> "The whining schoolboy, with his satchel, and shining morning face, creeping like snail unwillingly to school."
>
> AS YOU LIKE IT
> ACT 2 SCENE 7

Shakespeare may well be recalling his own school days when he describes a schoolboy's reluctance to go to school in the play *As You Like It*.

School started for William as early as 6:00 am and went on until 5:00 pm, with only a couple of breaks for breakfast and lunch. It was a long, hard day.

Boys who wanted to go to university or become lawyers, teachers or doctors had to learn to read, write and speak Latin.

Some of Shakespeare's ideas for characters and plots came from the ancient Roman writers he studied such as Seneca and the great poet Ovid. Shakespeare used *The Twin Brothers* by the Roman playwright Plautus as a basis for the plot of his *The Comedy of Errors*.

Seneca wrote stories about heroes who suffered and died. Scholars think his work influenced Shakespeare's more violent plays, including *Titus Andronicus* and *Richard III*.

19th-century illustration showing the unwilling schoolboy in *As You Like It*

When Shakespeare was 18, he married Anne Hathaway, a farmer's daughter. During the early years of their marriage, it's most likely that Anne moved into the Henley Street house with William and his family. When their first child, Susanna, was born, the house must have been very crowded. It would have become even more so once the twins Judith and Hamnet were born two years later.

Historians don't know what William did after leaving school. Since he probably wanted to write or act from an early age, he may have seen travelling players at a local inn yard and become stage-struck. What we do know is that he left his family in Stratford. This is a risk that not many men would take. By 1592 he was in London, well on his way towards fame and fortune.

Touring companies of actors performed on temporary stages, often in the yards of inns. Shakespeare was sure to have been one of the crowd who gathered to watch a play – an exciting event in a small town.

Anne Hathaway's cottage was once a large farmhouse.

London Bound

How Shakespeare must have marvelled when he first arrived in London. Rich and poor jostled each other as they made their way between tall houses that overhung the streets, shutting out light from above. Ladies picked their way carefully through mud and filth, and all about were the shouts of street traders. Often there would be a cry as someone realised they had been robbed or cheated by one of the many criminals who lurked, watching for the unwary.

In the 1500s London was a bustling, noisy city.

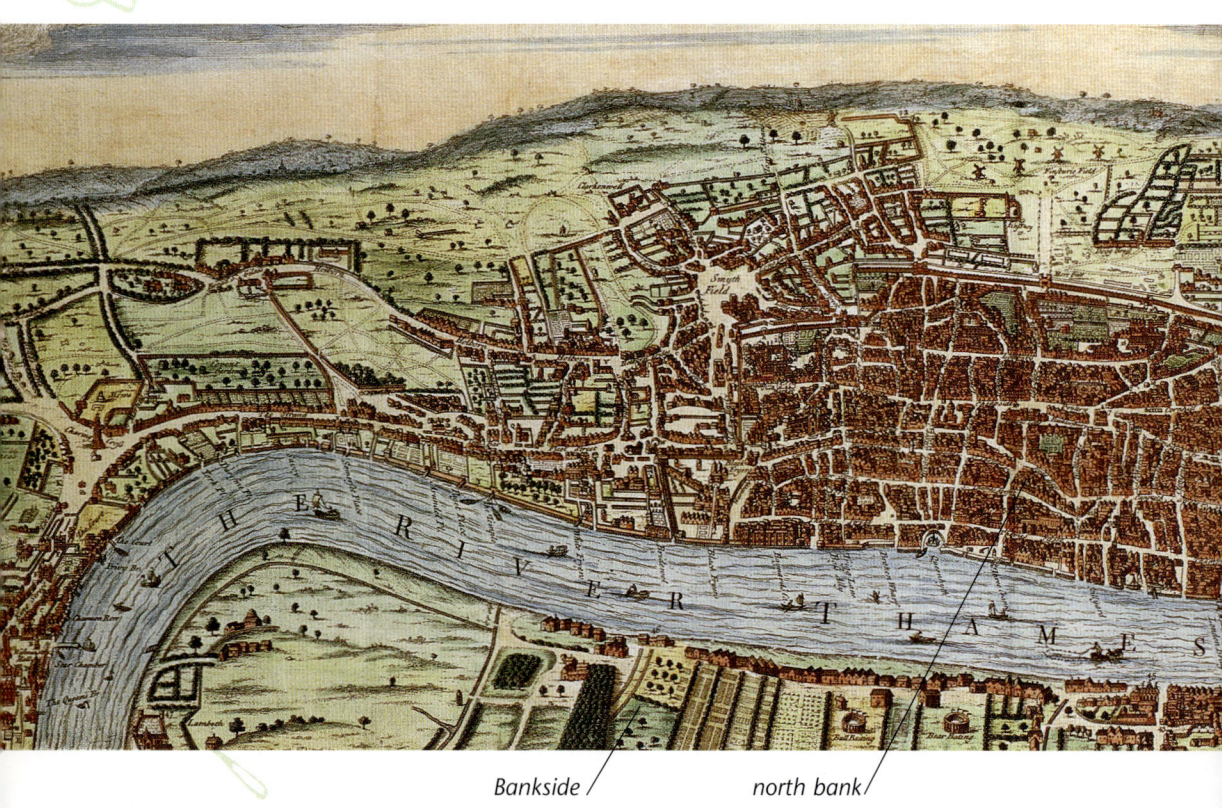

Bankside / north bank /

the Swan

the Rose

Shakespeare's ambition to act and write plays would have driven him to seek out London's playhouses. Four large public theatres were open in London in the late 16th century: the Theatre, the Swan, the Rose and the Curtain.

Besides plays, there was other entertainment in the city. Sports and gambling were popular pastimes, and usually the two were combined. Gamblers won or lost money on dice, cards and other betting games. Some games even involved contests between animals. All these sights and sounds must have fuelled the young Shakespeare's mind.

The Rose and the Swan theatres were built on Bankside. Like most early open-air playhouses, they were polygonal (multi-sided) in design.

London was built on the River Thames. Most people lived north of the river, though many theatres were built on the south bank of the river, known as Bankside.

Contests between bears and dogs were held in specially designed pits such as the Bear Garden on Bankside.

A company of actors perform at the royal court.

After Shakespeare arrived in London, he started writing plays and acting in a company of players. He studied other writers' work, listening and learning all the time. Soon he became successful – so successful, in fact, that an older playwright, Robert Greene, became jealous of him. Greene was one of a group of writers known as the "University Wits", and he thought that Shakespeare was inferior because he had not gone to a university. Greene called the new young writer an "upstart crow".

In fact, Shakespeare's career began at a time when the theatre was becoming more and more popular. One of its keenest supporters was Queen Elizabeth I herself.

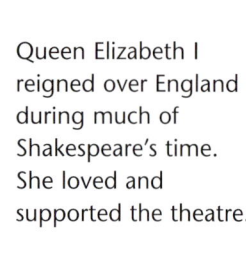

Queen Elizabeth I reigned over England during much of Shakespeare's time. She loved and supported the theatre.

Queen Elizabeth had been well educated. She knew Latin and Greek, and spoke French and Italian fluently, too. She loved literature and poetry, and there were many talented poets in her court.

Elizabeth liked to watch plays, and probably saw Shakespeare acting before she knew of him as a playwright. However, she never visited public playhouses. Instead companies of actors came to the Queen at her command and gave private performances for her and her court.

17th-century travelling library

> "A kingdom for a stage, princes to act
> And monarchs to behold the swelling scene."
>
> HENRY V, CHORUS

Queen Elizabeth, an ardent book lover, may have travelled with books like these.

Everything was written by hand, using a quill pen that was repeatedly dipped in ink. Shakespeare would have cut a new nib each time the pen's sharp edge wore out.

The public greeted Shakespeare's plays with delight, and his career blossomed. Other playwrights were also writing at the time, but Shakespeare's acting experience meant that he knew what dialogue and action would work well on stage. As he wrote, he could "hear" how an actor might speak his lines. He continued to take small parts in his own plays, but probably concentrated more on writing them.

Shakespeare was one of a group of successful writers who brought different experiences to their plays. Some were from the city, and some, like Shakespeare himself, had been raised in small country towns.

Shakespeare conveys powerful emotions through his use of dialogue and action. Here, in one of his greatest tragedies, *King Lear*, the king cries out in despair over the death of his daughter, Cordelia.

Shakespeare watched his rivals' plays and acted in some of them. He admired Christopher Marlowe in particular who wrote great dramatic tragedies. Some say that Marlowe greatly influenced Shakespeare's work.

Whether acting or watching, Shakespeare's imagination was constantly being nourished by the styles and ideas of his fellow playwrights and writers.

Acting in other playwrights' works, such as, perhaps, Thomas Kyd's *The Spanish Tragedy*, helped Shakespeare develop his own writing skills.

Christopher Marlowe was only 29 years old when he was stabbed to death in a London inn.

Shakespeare's first tragedy, *Titus Andronicus*, was inspired in part by the work of Christopher Marlowe.

Between 1592–1594, the Plague hit London and the theatres were closed. No one knew how the Plague spread, but the authorities decided it was not a good idea to go to crowded places. Anyone who could leave the city, did so. Actors left London and went on tour, possibly accidentally spreading the disease as they went.

Shakespeare used this time to concentrate on writing poetry. He dedicated two of his poems to Henry Wriothesley, Earl of Southampton, who paid him to write poetry and became his patron. Having an important nobleman supporting him helped people to take notice of Shakespeare's poetry.

Black rats ran freely through London's sewers and streets. Their fleas carried the dreaded plague.

"A plague o' both your houses!"

ROMEO AND JULIET
ACT 3 SCENE 1

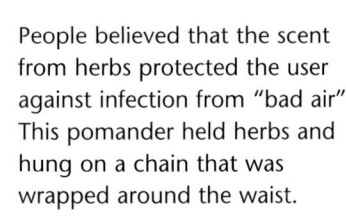

People believed that the scent from herbs protected the user against infection from "bad air". This pomander held herbs and hung on a chain that was wrapped around the waist.

On Stage

In 1594, when the plague epidemic had passed, the London playhouses reopened. William Shakespeare joined a company called the Lord Chamberlain's Men, and began writing about two plays a year for them. The Lord Chamberlain was the queen's cousin, and the company had plenty of chances to perform for Queen Elizabeth I. This was a great honour.

Shakespeare invested money in his company, becoming a "sharer". Sharers helped pay for costumes and wages, and in return, they received part of the profits. For the next few years, most of Shakespeare's working life was spent as one of the Lord Chamberlain's Men at the Theatre in north London. Shakespeare was both actor and writer for his company.

In 1597 the owner of the land on which the Theatre was built demanded that Shakespeare's company move out. So, over the Christmas holidays, the Lord Chamberlain's Men secretly dismantled the Theatre, plank by plank, carried it down to the river and placed it on a barge. Then they rebuilt it on the other side of the Thames.

Henry Carey, the Lord Chamberlain, was patron of Shakespeare's company.

Around this time, Shakespeare wrote one of his best-loved comedies, *Love's Labour's Lost*.

They renamed the new theatre the Globe. Like the old Theatre, it was open to the sky in the middle and surrounded by a thatched roof which protected the galleries of seats below. But if it rained the people standing in the middle who were called "groundlings", got wet.

The Globe could hold up to 3,000 people. Plays were held in the afternoon, since the theatre company needed daylight to light the stage. High above the theatre, a flag was flown whenever there was to be a performance.

The thatched roof sheltered three tiers of gallery seats from the rain. The Globe's thatched roof caught fire in 1613, burning it to the ground. The theatre was soon rebuilt, but with a tiled roof.

The balcony could represent an upper area in a play.

This reconstruction of Shakespeare's Globe in London gives a good idea of what the theatre looked like.

For a penny the theatre was open to a "groundling". For another penny the visitor could sit on one of the benches in the galleries. Richer people could sit in comfort in one of the gentlemen's rooms above the stage.

Theatre-going was a noisy, social event. Before the play started, people milled about, chatting, shouting, laughing and having fun. Plenty of drinking and eating went on, for there was no shortage of sellers of ale, fruit and nuts.

Shakespeare called his theatre the "wooden O", as the roof was open to the sky.

The stage ceiling was known as the Heavens. The underside was painted to look like a starry sky and may have depicted the signs of the Zodiac.

The lords' or gentlemen's rooms contained seats where wealthier playgoers could watch in comfort.

The columns in the Globe, which supported the Heavens, were painted to resemble marble. They also provided a hiding place for actors.

The Globe's stage projected, so the "groundlings" could stand around it to watch the play.

19

In this scene from a recent production of *Hamlet* at the new Globe theatre, a fight is broken up at the stage trapdoor, which represents a grave.

Elizabethan actors used very little scenery. Playwrights like William Shakespeare slipped clues as to setting and time of day into the actors' lines. When a character in *Henry VI* began, "Welcome, my lord, to this brave town of York", he needed no backdrop to set the scene. People knew from the speech that the scene was set in York. Similarly when an actor came on stage in broad daylight, carrying a lantern and peering about, everyone knew that it was night-time.

The stage and its roof provided opportunities for different effects. Characters were lowered from the Heavens. The trapdoor made it possible for a ghost to appear eerily or for an actor to suddenly disappear. Elizabethan audiences, who were not familiar with these tricks of the trade, must have often found it hard to believe their eyes.

Simple stage sets can be used to great comic effect. Here, characters hide behind a hedge in a modern production of *Twelfth Night* at the new Globe.

People expected music to be included in the performance. Musicians often sat in the gallery above the stage and played the accompaniments to the many songs that Shakespeare wrote into his plays.

Just as music helps create an atmosphere in cinema and on television today, so it did then. Drums and trumpets were played during a battle while lighter instruments like the lute were used in love scenes. In *The Taming of the Shrew*, however, a lute is used for a different purpose: Katherina cracks it across the head of one of her sister's admirers.

> "And with that word, she struck me on the head,
> And through the instrument my pate made way;"

THE TAMING OF THE SHREW ACT 2 SCENE 1

This drum is called a tabor. It would be struck with one hand while the other held the pipe.

Suitors often used a lute to serenade a lady.

petticoat | laced bodice | hooped farthingale | skirt

wig

make-up

A boy player needed help to get into a woman's dress for a performance. Once a boy was fully dressed, with wig and make-up applied, he would make a convincing woman.

Care and money were lavished on sumptuous theatrical costumes and wigs. Some were specially made while others were bought or donated to the company. Clothes were kept in a room immediately behind the stage, called the tiring house, where actors attired (dressed) themselves. Today it is called a dressing room.

Shakespeare wrote many different parts for women such as Juliet and the "weird sisters" of Macbeth. Boys or men played all parts because it was against the law for women to act on the stage. Shakespeare sometimes added confusion upon confusion, by creating situations where a man, playing a woman, would have to disguise himself as a man, as in, for example, *As You Like It*.

dress

The King's Men

In 1603 Elizabeth I died childless, and the crown passed to King James VI of Scotland, who then became James I of England. King James was enthusiastic about theatre and became a patron of the Lord Chamberlain's Men. From then on, the group called themselves the King's Men.

Many people think that Shakespeare wrote a play called *Macbeth*, which is set in Scotland, to please the Scottish ruler. In it, three "weird sisters" predict that the descendants of Banquo will become kings. Since King James believed he was a descendant of the real-life nobleman Banquo, Shakespeare may have guessed that the king would be pleased with this story.

King James I put even more money into supporting the theatre than Elizabeth did.

For fear of bad luck, this costume, from a production of *Macbeth*, will never be worn again. Ever since one of the cast members died in an early production of *Macbeth*, accidents have been linked to the play. Superstitious actors avoid mentioning it. Instead they call it "the Scottish play".

Shakespeare wrote his greatest tragedies for the Globe theatre. They explored great themes such as jealousy, revenge and death, and gave plenty of opportunity to stage dramatic fights.

Actors had to use swords and daggers properly. Fights and battles were expected to be realistic. After all, many gentlemen were well trained to fight with weapons. Incompetent fencing on stage wouldn't impress an audience, and they always made their feelings known towards the actor – perhaps with a carefully aimed apple.

Shakespeare's plays featured many sword fights and battles.

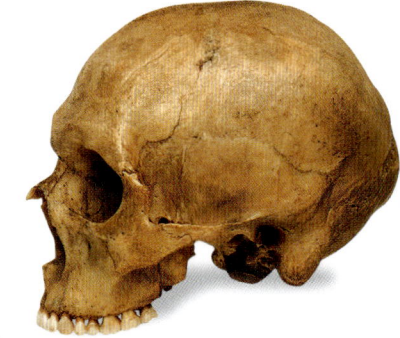

A skull is a theatrical symbol of death.

The tragedies feature main characters who have fatal flaws in their character. In *King Lear,* the King's vanity leads him to reject his youngest, and best-loved daughter, Cordelia. In *Othello,* the main character's terrible jealousy leads him to murder his wife.

In *Othello*, the main character's fatal flaw is jealousy.

Shakespeare was lucky to have some fine actors playing his leading roles. One of the most popular clowns of his day was William Kemp. He would have taken on some of Shakespeare's great comic roles such as Bottom in *A Midsummer Night's Dream*. Being a fine dancer, he would certainly have led the merry jig, a light-hearted dance that ends the play.

One of the most famous actors in Shakespeare's company was Richard Burbage. His father had owned the Theatre which Richard had helped dismantle and rebuild as the Globe. Some of Shakespeare's most powerful roles were written for the talented Burbage. He was praised for his ability to take on the great range and depth of Shakespeare's characters.

Shakespeare wrote *Hamlet* and *King Lear* with Richard Burbage in mind.

In *A Midsummer Night's Dream,* a weaver called Nick Bottom has his head turned into that of a donkey by a mischievous fairy, Puck. A further spell by Puck causes the Queen of the Fairies to fall madly in love with Bottom.

In 1608 the King's Men took on another playhouse called the Blackfriars Theatre. It was much smaller than the Globe and could hold perhaps 600–700 people.

The Blackfriars was an indoor theatre, lit by candles. The theatre was in a wealthier part of London than the Globe and was warm and dry, so the admission charges were higher. Only rich, fashionable people could afford to attend.

The King's Men continued to perform in the Globe, too, so they could still delight audiences both rich and poor.

Shakespeare wrote plays for the Blackfriars that had plenty of songs and music. These plays are called romances, and make greater use of magic and special effects.

The King's Men's new venture in 1608 appealed to a wealthier audience such as this well-dressed couple.

Shakespeare bought a house near the Blackfriars Theatre. This document gave him ownership and is signed by Shakespeare himself.

Shakespeare's romances include fantasy characters such as Prospero, a good magician, and the spirit, Ariel, in *The Tempest*. There is romance, too – in *Cymbeline*, the heroine's secret marriage is discovered and her husband is banished. After many exciting plot twists, the couple are happily reunited.

All Shakespeare's romances have happy endings. These plays combine love with music, magic and mystery. Audiences flocked to the little Blackfriars Theatre for a few hours of enchantment.

In *The Winter's Tale*, King Leontes' suspicion and mistrust of his wife, Hermione, lead to a long parting.

This modern production of *The Tempest* captures the magical quality of the play.

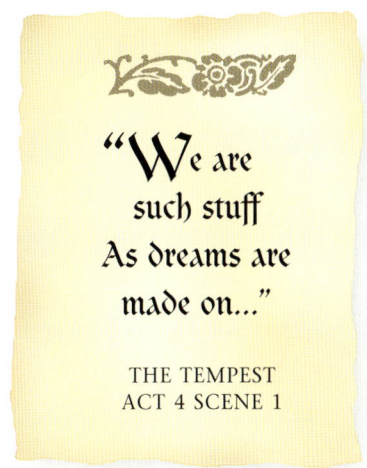

"We are such stuff As dreams are made on..."

THE TEMPEST
ACT 4 SCENE 1

27

This Elizabethan knot garden is on the site of Shakespeare's Stratford home in New Place.

Although Shakespeare spent much of his time in London, he often returned to Stratford-upon-Avon to visit his family. In 1596 tragedy struck when William's beloved son, Hamnet, died. He was only 11 years old. We don't know how he died, but we can imagine that William grieved terribly for him. In *King John* he wrote, "Grief fills the room up of my absent child".

A year later, Shakespeare bought a house called New Place. Here his wife and remaining children lived when he was working in London. In 1611 he joined Anne and his daughter Judith in New Place. (His eldest daughter Susanna was now married.)

Shakespeare returned to Stratford to retire, but he continued to write. His last play, *The Two Noble Kinsmen*, was written around 1613.

In Shakespeare's will, he left his "second-best bed" to his wife. The custom of the day was to give guests the best bed in the house.

Shakespeare enjoyed only a few years of retirement. Just one month after writing his will, William Shakespeare died on 23rd April 1616. He was 52 years old.

Shakespeare was buried in the graveyard of Holy Trinity Church, in Stratford-upon-Avon – very close to where he was born.

Shakespeare was very popular in his own lifetime, but he could never have known how many people would come to know and love his plays.

Shakespeare's last play was *The Two Noble Kinsmen*.

"His part is played, and though it were too short he did it well..."

THE TWO NOBLE KINSMEN
ACT 5 SCENE 6

When printing was a long, slow process, few people could afford to own a copy of a Shakespeare play.

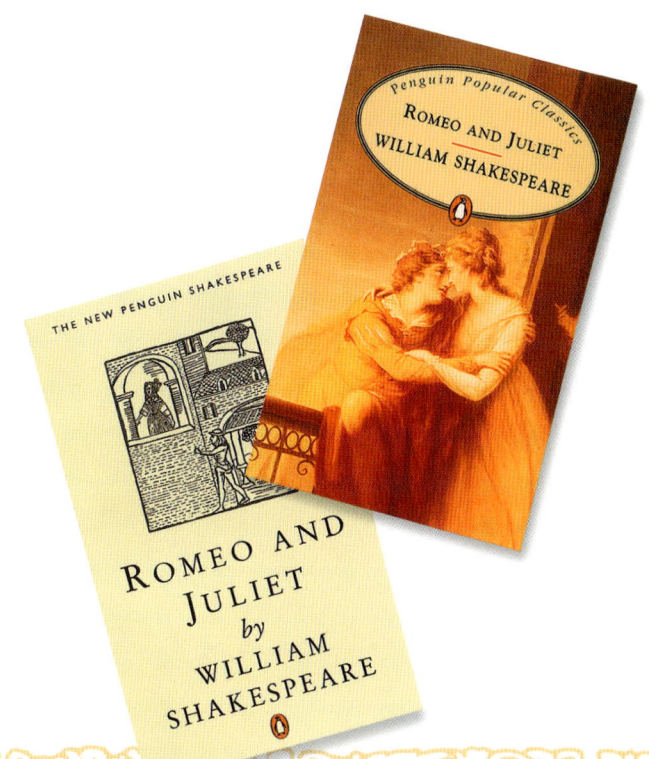

29

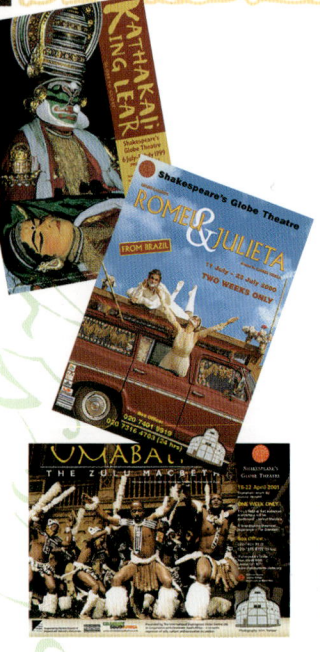

Shakespeare's plays have been made into films, stage musicals, ballets, operas and cartoons. In his plays Shakespeare explores common themes such as love and death. This makes his plays timeless and so they never go out of date. Shakespeare's stories and characters have inspired great works of art, and he is constantly being rediscovered – generation after generation.

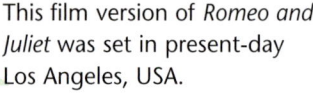

These posters show an Indian *King Lear*, a Brazilian *Romeo and Juliet* and an African *Macbeth*, all performed at the new Globe.

This film version of *Romeo and Juliet* was set in present-day Los Angeles, USA.

This film version of *Hamlet* starred Mel Gibson in the title role.

William Shakespeare himself is the subject of the popular film *Shakespeare in Love*.

Timeline

1564	William Shakespeare is born.
1582	Shakespeare marries Anne Hathaway.
1583	Daughter Susanna is born.
1585	Birth of twins, Judith and Hamnet.
1586–1587	Shakespeare possibly arrives in London.
1592	Shakespeare is established as an actor in London.
1594	Shakespeare is a leading member of the Lord Chamberlain's Men.
1596	John Shakespeare is granted a family coat of arms. Shakespeare's son, Hamnet, dies at the age of 11.
1597	Shakespeare buys New Place in Stratford-upon-Avon.
1598–1599	The Theatre is secretly dismantled, and the Globe Theatre is built.
1601	John Shakespeare dies. William, as his heir, inherits his family's coat of arms and becomes a "gentleman".
1603	Queen Elizabeth I dies, and James I of England becomes king. The Lord Chamberlain's Men become the King's Men.
1607	Shakespeare's daughter, Susanna, marries a physician, Dr John Hall.
1608	The King's Men take over the Blackfriars Theatre. Shakespeare's mother dies.
1611	Shakespeare returns to Stratford.
1613	The Globe theatre burns down when a prop cannon sets fire to the thatch. It is rebuilt.
1616	William Shakespeare dies in Stratford-upon-Avon.
1623	Anne Hathaway Shakespeare dies.

 ## THE PLAYS OF WILLIAM SHAKESPEARE

1590–93   The Two Gentlemen of Verona; Henry VI Part I; Henry VI Part II; Henry VI Part III; Richard III; Titus Andronicus; The Comedy of Errors; The Taming of the Shrew; Love's Labour's Lost

1594–96   A Midsummer Night's Dream; Romeo and Juliet; The Merchant of Venice; Richard II; King John

1596–99   Henry IV Part I; The Merry Wives of Windsor; Henry IV Part II; Much Ado About Nothing; Henry V

1596–99   Julius Caesar; As You Like It

1600–8   Hamlet; Troilus and Cressida; Twelfth Night; All's Well That Ends Well; Measure for Measure; Othello; King Lear; Macbeth; Antony and Cleopatra; Timon of Athens; Coriolanus

1609–11   Pericles; Cymbeline; The Winter's Tale; The Tempest

1612–14   Henry VIII; The Two Noble Kinsmen

No one is sure of the exact order in which Shakespeare's plays were written.

Index

As You Like It 8, 22, 32
boy actors 22
Burbage, Richard 25
Comedy of Errors, The 8, 32
Cymbeline 27, 32
Elizabeth I 12, 13, 17, 23, 31
Greene, Robert 12
Hamlet 20, 25, 30, 32
Hathaway, Anne 9, 28, 31
Henry V 13, 32
Henry VI 20, 32
James I 23, 31
Kemp, William 25
King John 28, 32
King Lear 14, 24, 25, 30, 32
King's Men 23, 26, 31
London 4, 9, 10, 11, 12, 15, 16, 17, 28, 31
Lord Chamberlain's Men 17, 23, 31

Love's Labour's Lost 17, 32
Macbeth 22, 23, 30, 32
Marlowe, Christopher 15
Midsummer Night's Dream, A 25, 32
Othello 24, 32
plague 16–17
playhouses 11, 17, 18, 24–26, 27, 31,
Richard III 8, 32
Romeo and Juliet 30, 32
Shakespeare, John 31
Stratford-upon-Avon 5, 7, 28–29
Taming of the Shrew, The 21, 32
Tempest, The 27, 32
Thames, River 11, 17
Titus Andronicus 8, 15, 32
Twelfth Night 20, 32
Two Noble Kinsmen, The 28, 29
Winter's Tale, The 27